iScience

Patterns and Textures:
Who Took the Pets?

by Emily Sohn and Laura Townsend

Chief Content Consultant
Edward Rock
Associate Executive Director, National Science Teachers Association

NORWOOD HOUSE PRESS
Chicago, Illinois

Norwood House Press
PO Box 316598
Chicago, IL 60631

For information regarding Norwood House Press, please visit our website at
www.norwoodhousepress.com or call 866-565-2900.

Special thanks to: Amanda Jones, Amy Karasick, Alanna Mertens and Terrence Young, Jr.

Editors: Jessica McCulloch, Barbara J. Foster, and Diane Hinckley
Designer: Daniel M. Greene
Production Management: Victory Productions, Inc.

Library of Congress Cataloging-in-Publication Data

Sohn, Emily.

Patterns and textures : who took the pets? / by Emily Sohn and Laura Townsend;

   p. cm.—(iScience readers)

   Summary: "Describes how little details around you can help solve mysteries
   and come up with new ideas. As readers use scientific inquiry to learn about
   patterns and textures and how often they benefit and are used in society, an
   activity based on real world situations challenges them to apply what they've
   learned in order to solve a puzzle"—Provided by publisher.

Includes bibliographical references and index.

ISBN-13: 978-1-59953-414-5 (library ed.: alk. paper)
ISBN-10: 1-59953-414-2 (library ed.: alk. paper)

1. Pattern perception—Juvenile literature. 2. Criminal investigation—Juvenile literature.
3. Logic puzzles—Juvenile literature. I. Townsend, Laura. II. Title. III. Series.

BF294.S64 2012
153.7—dc23
2011016657

Manufactured in the United States of America in North Mankato, Minnesota.

175N—072011

CONTENTS

Note to Caregivers:

Throughout this book, many questions are posed to the reader. Some are open-ended and ask what the reader thinks. Discuss these questions with your child and guide him or her in thinking through the possible answers and outcomes. There are also questions posed which have a specific answer. Encourage your child to read through the text to determine the correct answer. Most importantly, encourage answers grounded in reality while also allowing imaginations to soar. Information to help support you as you share the book with your child is provided in the back in the **Additional Notes** section.

Words that are **bolded** are defined in the glossary in the back of the book.

0011001000110111 0

Solving Problems, Cracking Mysteries

The world is full of details that are easy to miss. Look at and listen to what's around you, such as the veins of a leaf, the shape of an animal's paw print, pauses between words. Let your nose, hands, and ears help. You may start to notice **patterns.** You'll feel **textures.** These tools can help you solve mysteries. Pay attention. You might just save the day!

10000001100101010110
0001000000010001100
0101001000000011001
11101010110110101001
0101101101001000000
00000011100110110110 1
4 0110010101011100110 0

101100011011110111
1011101000010000001
010001011000010000
1110110110010101011
0001110101011001010
0010001101001011101
0111010101101111011
100011010 11011101 0
110101010 1 0110
00110100
110000100
1110110
1101100 1

Missing Animals!

You are an animal detective. You help people find missing pets. The phone in your office rings. It is the owner of a pet-food store. He keeps a cat, a dog, and a parrot in the store. He came in to check on the store around lunchtime. He found three empty cages. The worker is gone, too. The money is all there. This is a strange case. Can you help solve the mystery?

Where did the animals go?

What Is a Pattern?

This decorative ceiling is made up of many different patterns.

One way to make sense of the world is to look for patterns. A pattern can be a design that repeats itself. Or it can describe an event or action that happens over and over.

The picture on this page shows a ceiling with different patterns. Which parts show up again and again in the design?

Pattern Predictions

Detectives use patterns to solve crimes. Say a store has been robbed three weeks in a row. Each week, the robbery was on a Saturday night. This is a kind of pattern. It might make sense for the detectives to wait at the store on the fourth Saturday night. The detectives might then nab the robbers.

The pattern of a shoe print found at a crime scene can lead police to the right suspect.

You talk to the owner of the pet-food store. He says that his store has never been robbed before. He also adds that the worker has never left the cages open, and the animals have never escaped before. So maybe these aren't patterns to look for. But don't give up yet. There might be other patterns to find.

Seeing Nature

To solve the iScience Puzzle, you might need to think like a scientist. Scientists look for patterns all the time. Think about the colors in a rainbow. They always appear in the same order. Studying that pattern has taught scientists a lot about how light behaves.

The colors in a rainbow always appear in this order: red, orange, yellow, green, blue, indigo, and violet. To help you remember the color order, think of the name Roy G. Biv.

Animals have patterns, too. The store owner tells you that the missing dog is covered in spots. The cat sleeps every day from 9 a.m. to noon. The worker eats lunch at the same time every day. The parrot repeats the last word of every sentence it hears. These are all examples of patterns.

The owner thinks the animals disappeared around 11 in the morning. Does one puzzle choice make more sense or less sense than the others yet?

At the store, you find a few leaves near the empty parrot cage. They might be a clue. You want to look closely at the leaves. Every detail matters.

All leaves have veins that carry water. Veins in leaves are in one of three patterns. Knowing the pattern can help you find out what kind of leaves you are looking at.

Parallel venation is one vein pattern. Veins run from the bottom of the leaf to the top. They all go in the same direction. Many grasses have parallel veins.

As you can see here, the veins in grass leaves run in only one direction.

veins

Leaves with a large vein running through the middle have **pinnate venation.** Small veins branch off from the central vein. Apple tree leaves have pinnate venation.

central vein

small veins

Small veins in an apple tree leaf run from the central vein toward the edge of the leaf.

With **palmate venation,** veins spread out from the leaf's base. The veins look like fingers in a hand. Maple leaves have this pattern.

The veins in the maple leaf spread out from one point on the leaf's base.

You want to know which pattern the leaves in the store have. What you find might help later. Read on to learn more.

When you look at a leaf up close, you can see patterns and details. When you sweep your finger across the leaf, you can feel textures.

Rub-a-Dub

Go outside and find a flat, sturdy leaf. Place it on your desk with the bumpier side up. Put a piece of white paper on top of the leaf. Peel the paper off a crayon. Rub the side of the crayon on the paper. Move the crayon back and forth in only one direction. Make sure to color over the whole leaf.

Different textures in the leaf pick up color differently.
The pattern of the leaf shows in the rubbing.

You just made a leaf **rubbing.** It shows textures, patterns, and details. Can you think of anything besides leaves that you could make a rubbing of?

You find that the leaves in the store have parallel venation. That means they are probably a type of grass. How do you think the grass got into the store?

What Are Textures?

Your eyes aren't the only part of you that can look for clues. Your sense of touch can help, too. Texture describes the features of an object's surface. You might notice a smooth area on a rough floor. That would show you where lots of feet have walked. Feel around the room you're in. How many textures can you find?

How would you describe the textures of the objects shown? From top left: wood, leaves, grass, tree rings, leather, bricks.

Feel Your Way

Textures are at the root of some big inventions. Think about how the sense of touch can help people communicate.

Blind people read by using texture. They use their fingers to get the same information most of us get with our eyes.

❓ Did You Know?

In 1824, Louis Braille created a system that helped blind people read and write. In his system, patterns of raised dots make up units called cells. Each cell is a group of dots that stands for something. A cell might stand for a letter, a number, or a punctuation mark. Once they learn the cells, blind people can use their fingertips to read. Braille used texture to solve a big problem for people who could not see.

Seeing the Invisible

At the pet-food store, you might want to look for fingerprints. Fingerprints are marks left by tiny ridges on the tips of our fingers. Everyone has a different pattern of ridges on their fingers. We leave fingerprints on things we touch. But fingerprints are hard to see. Police have ways to find prints on surfaces. Later, they connect the prints to the person who left them behind.

A crime scene investigator is "dusting for prints." He brushes a powder onto surfaces where fingerprints might be. The powder sticks to the pattern of the prints. The investigator can then pick up the fingerprints with tape. Why does he wear gloves?

Carbon printing is one way to look more closely at fingerprints. This technique makes it easy to see fine textures. To make your own carbon print, rub a pencil back and forth on a blank sheet of paper. Press your thumb on the smudge. Your thumb should look almost black.

Put a piece of clear tape over the pencil mark on your thumb. Carefully peel the tape away. Your thumbprint is now caught on the tape. Press the tape on a white sheet of paper to preserve your thumbprint. How does your print compare to the prints of your friends or family members?

At the store, you find the worker's prints on the empty cages. You also find the owner's prints there. What does this clue tell you?

No two fingerprints are identical. That makes a fingerprint a very good way to identify someone. Can you find the differences between these two fingerprints?

 **Did You Know?**

No two people have the same fingerprints. Even identical twins have different patterns. Look at your thumbprint. What kind of patterns do you see? Do any of your friends have the same patterns?

21

Science at Work

Crime Scene Investigators

Crime scene investigators show up after a crime. They collect fingerprints and hair. They look for patterns and textures. They take all the clues to a **laboratory.** Then, they study this **evidence.** They can match clues to criminals. They don't always find an answer. But they often solve tough puzzles.

This investigator is marking evidence at a crime scene.

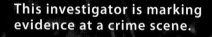

EVIDEN

DO NOT TOUCH

What Is a Mirror Image?

You've looked for patterns and textures. A mirror can also help you find clues. Lakes were the first mirrors. People looked into the water and saw their **reflections.** Today, there are glass mirrors in most homes and schools.

The first "mirrors" were ponds in which people saw reflections.

When you look in a mirror, you see things in reverse. The left is on the right. And the right is on the left. This is called a **mirror image.** A mirror image has **symmetry.** Some other things have symmetry as well. That means that two sides of an object are exact opposites of each other. A butterfly is a perfect example.

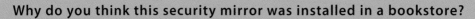

Detective Reflections

With a mirror, you can see what's going on behind you without turning your head. Mirrors help people see other cars when they drive. Mirrors in stores help workers watch shoppers.

Connecting to History

The Telescope

Telescopes look deep into space. They were invented in the early 1600s. The first versions used lenses to bend light. Like magnifying lenses, they made distant objects appear closer. Isaac Newton, an English scientist, added mirrors in the 1660s. Mirrors collect more light than your eyes can. Mirrored telescopes are used to see objects that are too dim to see with your eyes alone.

Over the years, telescope mirrors have grown bigger. With today's telescopes, we can see even dimmer stars, moons, and planets than Newton could see. These tools have helped answer many questions in science.

You are happy to
see the return of
the cat, the dog,
and the bird.

The Plot Thickens

There is a big mirror hanging in the pet-food store. From the cash register, you can use it to see the front door. As you look, you notice someone coming in. It's the missing worker! He's arriving with a dog, a cat, and a bird. There is grass on the bottom of his running shoes. You can hear the bird saying, "Lunch! Lunch!"

Look back at the puzzle choices. Think about the evidence you have.

Theory 1:

Someone broke into the store and took the animals. The worker went to get help and to look for the animals.

Evidence:

The money was still there. Nothing else seems amiss. This theory seems unlikely.

Who let the animals out?

Theory 2:

The animals' cage doors were left open during feeding and the animals escaped. The worker left to chase them.

Evidence:

The cat would have been napping and unaware. And the animals have never escaped before. This theory is probably not right.

Theory 3:

The worker took the animals and left.

Evidence:

There was grass on the floor of the store. The worker has grass on his shoes. You found his fingerprints on the cages, too. This theory fits.

You talk to the worker and find out the real story. He forgot his lunch at home. But he didn't want to leave the animals alone. So he took them with him. Mystery solved. Case closed!

In this book, you used many senses to solve a puzzle. See what else you can use your senses to do. At your next meal, put on a blindfold. Then, have someone bring you the food. Can you use your nose, mouth, and fingers to figure out what you're eating? What kinds of textures can you feel? What flavors can you taste? How might you use patterns to make good guesses about the menu?

What other mysteries can you solve around the house?

Could you guess what food this is if you were blindfolded?

GLOSSARY

carbon printing: a technique used to make fine textures visible.

evidence: something that helps to prove that an event did or did not happen.

laboratory: a place set up for science experiments.

mirror image: an image produced by a mirror. A mirror image is always reversed.

palmate venation: a leaf vein pattern in which veins start near the base of the leaf and branch out like fingers in a hand.

parallel venation: a leaf vein pattern in which veins run from the bottom of a leaf to the top and all go in the same direction.

patterns: 1. designs; how things are arranged.
2. usual ways of moving or acting.

pinnate venation: a leaf vein pattern in which one main vein runs up the center of the leaf and smaller veins branch out from the main vein.

reflections: images created after light strikes an object and reverses direction.

rubbing: an image of a textured surface created by placing paper over the surface and rubbing the paper with the side of a crayon.

symmetry: an arrangement in which the parts on opposite sides of a center line are the same.

textures: surface features of a material or object.

FURTHER READING

How Artists Use Patterns and Textures, by Paul Flux.
Heinemann, 2007.

Mirror, Mirror: A Book of Reversible Verse, by Marilyn Singer.
Dutton Juvenile, 2010.

Patterns in Nature, by Jennifer Rozines Roy and Greg Roy.
Marshall Cavendish, 2007.

Whose Fingerprints Are These? Crime-Solving Science Projects,
by Robert Gardner. Enslow Elementary, 2010.

Kidipede, Mosaics for Kids.
http://www.historyforkids.org/learn/arts/mosaic.htm

National Geographic Kids, Patterns in Nature.
http://kids.nationalgeographic.com/
kids/photos/gallery/patterns-in-nature/

ADDITIONAL NOTES

*The page references below provide answers to questions asked
throughout the book. Questions whose answers will vary
are not addressed.*

Page 11: The main flower part of the design is made of a center star surrounded by five identical large petals and five identical small petals. Each large petal is made of the same four smaller parts.

Page 20: Caption question: He wears gloves so that his fingerprints don't get mixed up with other prints at the crime scene.

Page 21: It tells you that both the owner and the worker touched the cages.

INDEX